P9-DZY-080

when the first baby laughed for the first time, its laugh broke into a thousand pieces, and they all went skipping about, and that was the beginning of fairies.   —J. M. Barrie, Scottish, 1860–1937, from Peter Pan

Fairyland

In Art and Poetry

Illustrated with art by Richard Doyle

THE METROPOLITAN MUSEUM OF ART

HENRY HOLT AND COMPANY
New York

741.64
D777f

The works of art reproduced in this book are chromolithographs
by Richard Doyle (English, 1824–1883) from *In Fairyland: A Series of Pictures from
the Elf-World*, published in London by Longmans, Green, Reader and Dyer in 1870.
The book is in the collections of the Department of Drawings and Prints,
The Metropolitan Museum of Art (Gift of Lincoln Kirstein, 1970 1970.565.74).

Published by The Metropolitan Museum of Art and Henry Holt and Company, LLC, 115 West
18th Street, New York, New York 10011. Distributed in Canada by H. B. Fenn and Company Ltd.

Copyright © 2001 by The Metropolitan Museum of Art

All rights reserved. No part of this publication may be reproduced or transmitted in any form or
by any means, electronic or mechanical, including photocopy, recording, or any information stor-
age or retrieval system, without permission in writing from the copyright owner and publisher.

Grateful acknowledgment is made to the following for permission to reproduce the copyrighted
material listed below. "Some One," by Walter de la Mare, from *The Complete Poems of Walter de la
Mare*, copyright © 1969 by Walter de la Mare, is reprinted by permission of the Literary Trustees of
Walter de la Mare and the Society of Authors as their representative. "Fairies," by Eleanor Farjeon,
from *Joan's Door*, copyright 1926, 1954 by Eleanor Farjeon, is reprinted by permission of David
Higham Associates and Harold Ober Associates. "I'd Love to Be a Fairy's Child," by Robert Graves,
from *Fairies and Fusiliers*, copyright 1917 by Robert Graves, is reprinted by permission of Carcanet
Press Limited. "Fairies," by Langston Hughes, from *The Collected Poems of Langston Hughes*, copyright © 1994 by the Estate of Langston Hughes, is reprinted by permission of Alfred A. Knopf,
a division of Random House, Inc., and Harold Ober Associates. Excerpts by William Shakespeare,
copyright © 1966 by the Cambridge text of *The Complete Works of William Shakespeare*, established
by John Dover Wilson, are reprinted by permission of Cambridge University Press. "Fairy Story,"
by Stevie Smith, from *The Collected Poems of Stevie Smith*, copyright © 1972 by Stevie Smith, is
reprinted by permission of New Directions Publishing Corp. and the Estate of James MacGibbon.
"The Stolen Child," by William Butler Yeats, from *Crossways*, copyright 1889 by William Butler
Yeats, is reprinted by permission of A. P. Watt Limited on behalf of Michael B. Yeats.

PACKARD LIBRARY

MAR 1 2 2008

COLUMBUS COLLEGE
OF
ART AND DESIGN

First Edition
Printed in Hong Kong

Produced by the Department of Special Publications, The Metropolitan Museum of Art:
Robie Rogge, Publishing Manager; William Lach, Editor;
Anna Raff, Designer; Tatiana Ginsberg, Assistant Production Manager.
All photography by The Metropolitan Museum of Art Photograph Studio

Visit the Museum's Web site: www.metmuseum.org

ISBN 0-87099-995-8 (MMA)
10 09 08 07 06 05 04 03 02   5 4 3

ISBN 0-8050-7006-0 (Henry Holt)
3 5 7 9 10 8 6 4 2

Library of Congress Cataloging-in-Publication Data
Fairyland : in art and poetry / edited by William Lach ; art by Richard Doyle.
p. cm.
ISBN 0-87099-995-8 (MMA).—ISBN 0-8050-7006-0 (Henry Holt)
1. Fairy poetry, English. 2. Fairy poetry, American. 3. Fairies in art. [1. Fairies—Poetry.]
I. Lach, William, 1968– II. Doyle, Richard, 1824–1883, ill.

PR508.F34 F35 2001
398.2—dc21

2001030714

Contents

Introduction

hat is it about Richard Doyle's fairies that makes them so charming? Is it the precise, beetles-and-botany settings he places them in? Or is it their actions, as devious as they are delightful, and as unpredictable as those of real children? (For every sweet-faced fairy dancing with a butterfly or squirrel, there's a chubby, scowling elf-baby tormenting the same.)

The fairy lithographs reproduced here were first published in 1870, in the book *In Fairyland: A Series of Pictures from the Elf-World*, loosely paired with a poem by William Allingham. Fourteen years later, Doyle's irrepressible artwork was published again, only this time in bits and pieces, alongside a discursive tale concocted by Andrew Lang, author of the popular color-fairy books.

Perhaps the chorus of poets in this collection, working in nursery rhymes, ballads, blank verse, and songs, ranging over four hundred years and much of the English-speaking world, best suits Doyle's riotous vision. Here, a parade of lake fairies illuminates the bewitching imagery of William Butler Yeats's "The Stolen Child"; a rising moon reveals the mysterious prankster of Walter de la Mare's "Some One"; and three slapstick elves act out Vachel Lindsay's fanciful "An Explanation of the Grasshopper." In short, these are fairies that behave just as real children would, if only they were small enough.

—William Lach

Dreams

Beyond, beyond the mountain line,
    The grey-stone and the boulder,
Beyond the growth of dark green pine,
    That crowns its western shoulder,
There lies that fairy-land of mine,
    Unseen of a beholder.

Its fruits are all like rubies rare;
    Its streams are clear as glasses;
There golden castles hang in air,
    And purple grapes in masses,
And noble knights and ladies fair
    Come riding down the passes.

Ah me! they say if I could stand
    Upon those mountain ledges,
I should but see on either hand
    Plain fields and dusty hedges;
And yet I know my fairy-land
    Lies somewhere o'er their edges.

—*Cecil Frances Alexander, English, 1818–1895*

Ariel's Song

Where the bee sucks, there suck I.
In a cowslip's bell I lie.
There I couch, when owls do cry.
On the bat's back I do fly
After summer merrily....
Merrily, merrily, shall I live now,
Under the blossom that hangs on the bough.

—*William Shakespeare, English, 1564–1616*

The Leprahaun

In a shady nook one moonlit night,
  A leprahaun I spied
In scarlet coat and cap of green,
  A cruiskeen by his side.
'Twas tick, tack, tick, his hammer went,
  Upon a weeny shoe,
And I laughed to think of a purse of gold,
  But the fairy was laughing too.

With tip-toe step and beating heart,
  Quite softly I drew nigh.
There was mischief in his merry face,
  A twinkle in his eye;
He hammered and sang with tiny voice,
  And sipped the mountain dew;
Oh! I laughed to think he was caught at last,
  But the fairy was laughing, too.

As quick as thought I grasped the elf,
  "Your fairy purse," I cried,
"My purse?" said he, "'tis in her hand,
  That lady by your side."
I turned to look, the elf was off,
  And what was I to do?
Oh! I laughed to think what a fool I'd been,
  And, the fairy was laughing too.

—Robert Dwyer Joyce, Irish, 1830–1883

The Fairies in New Ross

When moonlight
Near midnight
Tips the rock and waving wood;

When moonlight
Near midnight
Silvers o'er the sleeping flood;

When yew-tops
With dew-drops
Sparkle o'er deserted graves;

'Tis then we fly
Through welkin high,
Then we sail o'er yellow waves.

—Anonymous, Irish, early 19th century

from *The Fairies*

Up the airy mountain,
    Down the rushy glen,
We daren't go a-hunting
    For fear of little men;
Wee folk, good folk,
    Trooping all together;
Green jacket, red cap,
    And white owl's feather!

Down along the rocky shore
    Some make their home,
They live on crispy pancakes
    Of yellow tide-foam;
Some in the reeds
    Of the black mountain lake,
With frogs for their watch-dogs,
    All night awake.

High on the hill-top
    The old King sits;
He is now so old and grey
    He's nigh lost his wits.
With a bridge of white mist,
    Columbkill he crosses,
On his stately journeys
    From Slieveleague to Rosses;
Or going up with music
    On cold starry nights,
To sup with the Queen
    Of the gay Northern Lights.

By the craggy hill-side,
    Through the mosses bare,
They have planted thorn-trees
    For pleasure here and there.
Is any man so daring
    As dig them up in spite,
He shall find their sharpest thorns
    In his bed at night.

Up the airy mountain,
    Down the rushy glen,
We daren't go a-hunting
    For fear of little men;
Wee folk, good folk,
    Trooping all together;
Green jacket, red cap,
    And white owl's feather!

—*William Allingham, Irish, 1824–1889*

Fairy Things

Grey lichens, mid thy hills of creeping thyme,
Grow like to fairy forests hung with rime;
And fairy money-pots are often found
That spring like little mushrooms out of ground,
Some shaped like cups and some in slender trim
Wineglasses like, that to the very rim
Are filled with little mystic shining seed;
We thought our fortunes promising indeed,
Expecting by and by ere night to find
Money ploughed up of more substantial kind.

Acres of little yellow weeds,
The wheat-field's constant blooms,
That ripen into prickly seeds
For fairy curry-combs,
To comb and clean the little things
That draw their nightly wain;
And so they scrub the beetle's wings
Till he can fly again.

And flannel felt for the beds of the queen
From the soft inside of the shell of the bean,
Where the gipsies down in the lonely dells
Had littered and left the plundered shells.

—*John Clare, English, 1793–1864*

I'd Love to Be a Fairy's Child

Children born of fairy stock
Never need for shirt or frock,
Never want for food or fire,
Always get their heart's desire:
Jingle pockets full of gold,
Marry when they're seven years old.
Every fairy child may keep
Two strong ponies and ten sheep;
All have houses, each his own,
Built of brick or granite stone;
They live on cherries, they run wild—
I'd love to be a fairy's child.

—Robert Graves, English, 1895–1985

Fairy Story

I went into the wood one day
And there I walked and lost my way

When it was so dark I could not see
A little creature came to me

He said if I would sing a song
The time would not be very long

But first I must let him hold my hand tight
Or else the wood would give me a fright

I sang a song, he let me go
But now I am home again there is nobody I know.

—Stevie Smith, English, 1902–1971

La Belle Dame sans Merci

"O what can ail thee, knight-at-arms,
Alone and palely loitering?
The sedge has withered from the lake,
And no birds sing.

"O what can ail thee, knight-at-arms,
So haggard and so woe-begone?
The squirrel's granary is full,
And the harvest's done.

"I see a lily on thy brow
With anguish moist and fever dew,
And on thy cheeks a fading rose
Fast withereth too."

"I met a lady in the meads,
Full beautiful—a faery's child,
Her hair was long, her foot was light,
And her eyes were wild.

"I made a garland for her head,
	And bracelets too, and fragrant zone;
She looked at me as she did love,
	And made sweet moan.

"I set her on my pacing steed
	And nothing else saw all day long,
For sidelong would she bend, and sing
	A faery's song.

"She found me roots of relish sweet,
	And honey wild, and manna dew,
And sure in language strange she said—
	'I love thee true.'

"She took me to her elfin grot,
	And there she wept, and sighed full sore,
And there I shut her wild wild eyes
	With kisses four.

"And there she lullèd me asleep,
    And there I dreamed—Ah! woe betide!
The latest dream I ever dreamed
    On the cold hill's side.

"I saw pale kings and princes too,
    Pale warriors, death-pale were they all;
They cried—'La Belle Dame sans Merci
    Hath thee in thrall!'

"I saw their starved lips in the gloam,
    With horrid warning gapèd wide,
And I awoke and found me here,
    On the cold hill's side.

"And this is why I sojourn here,
    Alone and palely loitering,
Though the sedge is withered from the lake
    And no birds sing."

—John Keats, English, 1795–1821

I Know a Bank Where the Wild Thyme Blows

I know a bank where the wild thyme blows,
Where oxlips and the nodding violet grows,
Quite over-canopied with luscious woodbine,
With sweet musk-roses, and with eglantine:
There sleeps Titania sometime of the night,
Lulled in these flowers with dances and delight;
And there the snake throws her enamelled skin,
Weed wide enough to wrap a fairy in.

—*William Shakespeare, English, 1564–1616*

The Flowers

All the names I know from nurse:
Gardener's garters, Shepherd's purse,
Bachelor's buttons, Lady's smock,
And the Lady Hollyhock.

Fairy places, fairy things,
Fairy woods where the wild bee wings,
Tiny trees for tiny dames—
These must all be the fairy names!

Tiny woods below whose boughs
Shady fairies weave a house;
Tiny tree-tops, rose or thyme,
Where the braver fairies climb!

Fair are grown-up people's trees,
But the fairest woods are these;
Where if I were not so tall,
I should live for good and all.

—Robert Louis Stevenson, Scottish, 1850–1894

The Fairies in the Sunshine

The little sunshine fairies
Are out on sunny days.
They gaily go a-dancing
Along the country ways.

They paint the flower faces,
The leaves of forest trees,
And tint the little grasses
All waving in the breeze.

(One painting tiger lilies,
Who runs away and goes
To play awhile with baby,
Puts speckles on his nose!!)

They color all the apples
And work for days and weeks
To make the grapes bloom purple
And paint the peaches' cheeks.

Ah! There's a tiny fairy!
She's in the garden bed!
It's little Ray O' Sunshine
Who makes the roses red.

—*Laura Ingalls Wilder, American, 1867–1957*

Echo Song

The splendour falls on castle walls
    And snowy summits old in story:
The long light shakes across the lakes,
    And the wild cataract leaps in glory.
Blow, bugle, blow, set the wild echoes flying,
Blow, bugle; answer, echoes, dying, dying, dying.

O hark, O hear! how thin and clear,
    And thinner, clearer, farther going!
O sweet and far from cliff and scar
    The horns of Elfland faintly blowing!
Blow, let us hear the purple glens replying:
Blow, bugle; answer, echoes, dying, dying, dying.

O love, they die in yon rich sky,
　　They faint on hill or field or river:
Our echoes roll from soul to soul,
　　And grow for ever and for ever.
Blow, bugle, blow, set the wild echoes flying,
And answer, echoes, answer, dying, dying, dying.

—Alfred, Lord Tennyson, English, 1809–1892

from *The Fairy Nurse*

Sweet babe! a golden cradle holds thee,
And soft the snow-white fleece enfolds thee;
In airy bower I'll watch thy sleeping,
Where branchy trees to the breeze are sweeping.
    Shuheen, sho, lulo lo!

Within our magic halls of brightness,
Trips many a foot of snowy whiteness;
Stolen maidens, queens of fairy—
And kings and chiefs a sluagh-shee airy.
    Shuheen, sho, lulo lo!

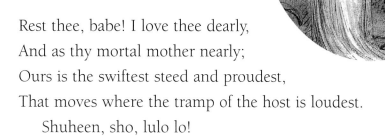

Rest thee, babe! I love thee dearly,
And as thy mortal mother nearly;
Ours is the swiftest steed and proudest,
That moves where the tramp of the host is loudest.
    Shuheen, sho, lulo lo!

Rest thee, babe! for soon thy slumbers
Shall flee at the magic koelshie's numbers;
In airy bower I'll watch thy sleeping,
Where branchy trees to the breeze are sweeping.
    Shuheen, sho, lulo lo!

—Edward Walsh, Irish, 1805–1850

Queen Mab

O then I see Queen Mab hath been with you.
She is the fairies' midwife, and she comes
In shape no bigger than an agate-stone
On the fore-finger of an alderman,
Drawn with a team of little atomi
Over men's noses as they lie asleep.
Her chariot is an empty hazel-nut,
Made by the joiner squirrel or old grub
Time out o' mind the fairies' coachmakers:
Her waggon-spokes made of long spinners' legs,
The cover of the wings of grasshoppers,
Her traces of the smallest spider-web,
Her collars of the moonshine's watery beams,
Her ship of cricket's bone, the lash of film;

Her waggoner a small grey-coated gnat,
Not half so big as a round little worm
Pricked from the lazy finger of a maid.
And in this state she gallops night by night
Through lovers' brains, and then they dream of love;
O'er courtiers' knees, that dream on curtsies straight;
O'er lawyers' fingers who straight dream on fees;
O'er ladies' lips, who straight on kisses dream....

—*William Shakespeare, English, 1564–1616*

Some One

Some one came knocking
    At my wee, small door;
Some one came knocking,
    I'm sure—sure—sure;
I listened, I opened,
    I looked to left and right,
But nought there was a-stirring
    In the still dark night;
Only the busy beetle
    Tap-tapping in the wall,
Only from the forest
    The screech-owl's call,
Only the cricket whistling
    While the dewdrops fall,
So I know not who came knocking,
    At all, at all, at all.

—*Walter de la Mare, English, 1873–1956*

from *The Stolen Child*

Where dips the rocky highland
Of Sleuth Wood in the lake,
There lies a leafy island
Where flapping herons wake
The drowsy water rats;
There we've hid our faery vats,
Full of berries,
And of reddest stolen cherries.
Come away, O human child!
To the waters and the wild
With a faery, hand in hand,
For the world's more full of weeping than you can understand.

Where the wave of moonlight glosses
The dim grey sands with light,
Far off by furthest Rosses
We foot it all the night,
Weaving olden dances,
Mingling hands and mingling glances
Till the moon has taken flight;
To and fro we leap
And chase the frothy bubbles,
While the world is full of troubles
And is anxious in its sleep.

Come away, O human child!
To the waters and the wild
With a faery, hand in hand,
For the world's more full of weeping than you can understand.

Where the wandering water gushes
From the hills above Glen-Car,
In pools among the rushes
That scarce could bathe a star,
We seek for slumbering trout
And whispering in their ears
Give them unquiet dreams;
Leaning softly out
From ferns that drop their tears
Over the young streams,
Come away, O human child!
To the waters and the wild
With a faery, hand in hand,
For the world's more full of weeping than you can understand.

—William Butler Yeats, Irish, 1865–1939

An Explanation of the Grasshopper

The Grasshopper, the Grasshopper,
I will explain to you:
He is the Brownies' racehorse,
The Fairies' Kangaroo.

—Vachel Lindsay, American, 1879–1931

Fairies

Out of the dust of dreams
Fairies weave their garments.
Out of the purple and rose of old memories
They make rainbow wings.
No wonder we find them such marvellous things!

—*Langston Hughes, American, 1902–1967*

The Fairy Folk

Come cuddle close in daddy's coat
    Beside the fire so bright,
And hear about the fairy folk
    That wander in the night.
For when the stars are shining clear,
    And all the world is still,
They float across the silver moon
    From hill to cloudy hill.

Their caps of red, their cloaks of green,
    Are hung with silver bells,
And when they're shaken with the wind,
    Their merry ringing swells.
And riding on the crimson moths
    With black spots on their wings,
They guide them down the purple sky
    With golden bridle rings.

They love to visit girls and boys
    To see how sweet they sleep,
To stand beside their cosy cots
    And at their faces peep.
For in the whole of fairy land
    They have no finer sight
Than little children sleeping sound
    With faces rosy bright.

On tiptoe crowding round their heads,
    When bright the moonlight beams,
They whisper little tender words
    That fill their minds with dreams;
And when they see a sunny smile,
    With lightest fingertips
They lay a hundred kisses sweet
    Upon the ruddy lips.

And then the little spotted moths
    Spread out their crimson wings,
And bear away the fairy crowd
    With shaking bridle rings.
Come, bairnies, hide in daddy's coat,
    Beside the fire so bright—
Perhaps the little fairy folk
    Will visit you tonight.

—*Robert M. Bird, American, 1803–1854*

The Fairies' Lullaby

You spotted snakes, with double tongue,
    Thorny hedgehogs, be not seen;
Newts and blind-worms do no wrong,
    Come not near our Fairy Queen.
    Philomele, with melody,
    Sing in our sweet lullaby,
            Lulla, lulla, lullaby,
            Lulla, lulla, lullaby,
    Never harm,
    Nor spell, nor charm,
Come our lovely lady nigh.
So good night, with lullaby.

Weaving spiders come not here:
    Hence you long-legged spinners, hence:
Beetles black approach not near:
    Worm nor snail do no offence.
    Philomele, with melody,
    Sing in our sweet lullaby,
            Lulla, lulla, lullaby,
            Lulla, lulla, lullaby,
    Never harm,
    Nor spell, nor charm,
Come our lovely lady nigh.
So good night, with lullaby.

—William Shakespeare, English, 1564–1616

Fairies

Don't go looking for fairies,
    They'll fly away if you do.
You never can see the fairies
    Till they come looking for you.

—Eleanor Farjeon, English, 1881–1965